I044225

<u>INDEX</u>

Introduction

33 years ago, three spectacular attacks in Beirut over an 18-month period announced the debut of a potent new force in Lebanon—the Shiite Hezbollah militia— and defined its relationship with the United States for years to come. The October 1983 bombings of Multinational Force bases took the lives of 241 Americans and 58 French.

Beirut, a city battered by war, was experiencing a period of relative calm in fall 1983. U.S. diplomats and soldiers were still coming to terms with the suicide bombing that struck the U.S. embassy in April, and U.S. Marines wore their combat uniforms everywhere they went—even to social events and diplomatic functions. But to the U.S. Marine commander on site, the threat environment seemed to have eased somewhat. The embassy bombing was seen as an outlier event. Marines were free to roam the city and were interacting with Lebanese children in public without fear of ambush. Beirut was under a cease-fire, and hopes were high for Syrian reconciliation talks. It was the quiet before the storm.

The U.S. embassy was bombed on April 18, 1983, killing 63, including 17 Americans. The driver of the explosive-filled van entered the embassy compound, slowed to navigate a sharp left turn down a cobblestone lane, and then accelerated and crashed into the embassy's front wall. The seven-floor embassy complex was engulfed in clouds of black smoke that hid the bodies of Lebanese security guards and American government workers torn apart by the blast. Among the dead were the top American intelligence officials stationed in Lebanon, including the CIA's chief Middle East analyst, Robert C. Ames.

In the early hours of October 23, 1983, a young Lebanese man from a Shi'a family awoke, said his morning prayers, and drank tea. In a suburb overlooking the marine barracks, his superiors shared a few final thoughts with him, after which a senior cleric blessed him before he drove off in a yellow Mercedes truck. At 6:22 a.m., he rammed the explosive-laden truck through the guard post at the entrance to the U.S. Marine Battalion Headquarters Building in Beirut. The blast decimated the four-story, concrete, steel- reinforced structure —considered one of the strongest buildings in Lebanon at the time. A dense, gray ash cloud engulfed the area as emergency vehicles rushed to the scene. Those soldiers lucky enough to escape serious injury quickly mobilized to rescue their fellow marines, sifting through "dust-covered body parts, moaning wounded and dazed survivors." Seconds later, a nearly identical attack targeted the French Multinational Force (MNF) building less than four miles away. Those attacks left 241 Americans and 58 French dead. Less than a year later, on September 20, 1984, the U.S. embassy annex was bombed, killing 24.

Lebanon's devastating civil war, which lasted from 1975 to 1990, hardened divisions among the country's various sectarian communities. Against this backdrop, the 1982 Israeli invasion and subsequent occupation of southern Lebanon created the space in which Iranian diplomats and agents could help fashion the unified entity Hezbollah from a motley crew of Shi'a militias and groups. Another turning point in the 1980s involved militants targeting not only fellow Lebanese but also the international forces dispatched as peacekeepers to provide the war-torn country with a measure of security. Over time, Hezbollah and Iran's interests in driving foreign forces out of Lebanon would expand from attacks targeting Western interests in Lebanon to attacks on Western interests abroad.

Over a nine-month period in 1985, the CIA calculated, Iran's Lebanese proxy groups were responsible for at least 24 international terrorist incidents. Such targets were popular given Iran's efforts to dissuade countries from arming and supporting Iraq in its ongoing, costly war against the Islamic Republic. Heeding Iran's call to carry out attacks beyond Lebanon's borders, Hezbollah would engage in plots throughout the Middle East. By February 1985, the CIA would warn that "Iranian-sponsored terrorism" presented the greatest threat to U.S. personnel and facilities in the region. Inevitably some of the Hezbollah operatives sent to conduct attacks in places like Kuwait were caught, leading Hezbollah to plot bombings, hijackings, and other operations in places as diverse as Germany and the Republic of the Congo in an effort to secure the release of jailed comrades.

The U.S. government had little doubt about who was behind the 1984 attack, even before crime-scene analysis and sensitive source reporting began to flow in. Writing just days after the second embassy bombing, the CIA noted that "*an overwhelming body of circumstantial evidence points to the Hizballah, operating with Iranian support under the cover name of Islamic Jihad.*"

For one thing, the suicide vehicle bomb employed had become a trademark of the group. And, the CIA added at the time, "*Shia fundamentalists are the only organized terrorists in Lebanon likely to willingly sacrifice their lives in such an* attack." Following the bombing, two callers claimed responsibility in the name of Hezbollah's Islamic Jihad Organization (IJO). Several times in the year to follow, the CIA noted, anonymous callers in Beirut warned that the IJO planned to continue attacking U.S. interests. FBI forensic investigators determined that the marine barracks bombing was not only the deadliest terrorist attack then to have targeted Americans, it was also the single-largest non-nuclear explosion on earth since World War II.

Composed of at least 18,000 pounds of explosives— the equivalent of six tons of dynamite — the bomb demolished the four-story building on the fringe of the Beirut Airport campus, leaving behind a crater at least 13 feet deep and 30 feet wide. So many marines, sailors, and soldiers perished that day that the base ran out of body bags. At the French MNF building, the deaths of 58 French paratroopers marked the French military's highest death toll since the Algerian war ended in 1962. The eight-story building where the paratroopers were staying was literally upended by the blast.

Imad Mughniyeh, the Hezbollah operational leader and terrorist mastermind, and his brother-in-law and cousin, Mustapha Badreddine, reportedly not only watched the marine barracks bombing through binoculars from a perch atop a nearby building overlooking their neighborhood but also coordinated it. In February 1998, Lebanon's highest court announced plans to try Hezbollah's first secretary-general, Subhi al-Tufayli, for his role in the marine barracks bombing, among other crimes. At the time, the CIA assessed that Iran, Syria, and Hezbollah would likely help Tufayli escape so he could not "implicate them in a variety of illegal activities, including terrorist operations against U.S. citizens." He was never tried. Another suspect was Mohammad Hussein Fadlallah, a leader of the Lebanese Shi'a community often described as one of Hezbollah's founding spiritual figures.

In 1986, the CIA reported that Fadlallah "has long been recognized as the spiritual leader of and political spokesman for Lebanon's Shia Hezbollah." Fadlallah's stature, the CIA added, grew "along with Hizballah's political and military influence." Fadlallah "benefited from and contributed to the growing extremism in the Shia community by his bold sermons attacking Israel and, later, the presence of the Multinational Force in Lebanon." Lebanese Shi'a were inspired by the Iranian revolution to seek an Islamic state in Lebanon, and Fadlallah valued his ties to Iran, in large part because of the significant military, financial, and political assistance Tehran provided to Hezbollah. This assistance helped forge a powerful and potent militant Shi'a group out of several smaller groups.

But over time Fadlallah's relationship with Iran changed. Fadlallah never fully embraced the Iranian revolutionary concept of velayat-e faqih (rule of the jurisprudent), which, according to a 1986 U.S. intelligence report, "*virtually equates Khomeini with the Mahdi— the 12th Imam who is in occultation.*" As much as Fadlallah sought an Islamic state in Lebanon, U.S. intelligence analysts concluded he also recognized the need to maintain the country's religious diversity within an Islamic context. But other, more radical voices within Hezbollah, like the up-and-coming security official Hassan Nasrallah, the CIA warned, promoted a maximalist program in which an Islamic republic in Lebanon would presage a pan-Islamic movement spanning the entire Muslim world. "In our view," the analysts wrote in 1988, "*Nasrallah does not represent the mainstream of the movement.*" Four years later Nasrallah would rise to the leadership of Hezbollah, moving the group's mainstream sharply to the right.

Modus Operandi

Hezbollah operatives are expert at gaining entry to their target locations through extremely subtle infiltration. This should not surprise, as many Hezbollah operatives receive sophisticated training both in Lebanon and in Iran from Iran's Ministry of Intelligence and Security (MOIS) and Islamic Revolutionary Guard Corp (IRGC) al-Quds Brigades. Members of a Hezbollah cell operating in Singapore in the late 1990s and into 2000 entered using a visa-waiver program similar to the one that recently suspended in the United States. Once they arrived, they quickly married local women to legalize their presence.

Members of a Hezbollah cell in North Carolina, which raised significant sums of money for the group from the proceeds of an elaborate cigarette smuggling scam, entered the U.S. from South America using false documents, entered into sham marriages in Cyprus, and conducted their activities under multiple identities.

Hezbollah cells are frequently involved in fundraising activities, even if they are primarily operational cells. Hezbollah cells raise funds through charities acting as front organizations as well as via criminal activity like cigarette smuggling, drug production and smuggling, and credit card or other types of fraud.

Hezbollah networks organize regular parlor meetings held in members' homes where a collection basket is passed around after watching Hezbollah propaganda videos, usually produced by al-Manar, the group's satellite television network. For example, the Charlotte network gathered on a regular basis to watch videos of live Hezbollah bombings in southern Lebanon before the Israeli withdrawal then collected donations to support such activities.

Contrary to conventional wisdom, Hezbollah is extremely adept at recruiting members from local populations in areas where they have networks on the ground. In Russia, Hezbollah operatives recruited Sunni Palestinian students studying at Russian universities, while in Uganda they recruited Ugandan Shia students and sent them to study abroad at an Iranian university where they also received military training together with Lebanese recruits in the use of small arms, making explosives, counter-interrogation techniques and escape planning. Before returning home, the Ugandans were provided fictitious covers and instructed to establish an operational network in Uganda.

In Southeast Asia, members of the network that was behind an attempt to bomb the Israeli embassy in Bangkok in 1994, as well as a series of other plots throughout the 1990s, were almost entirely Sunni. The leader of the network, Pandu Yudhawitna, was himself recruited by MOIS officers stationed in Malaysia in the early 1980s, and only later became the Southeast Asian point-man for Hezbollah operations and support activities there.

Hezbollah cells are adept multi-taskers, responsible for a variety of logistical, financial and operational duties. They raise funds, recruit new members, conduct preoperational surveillance, provide logistical support, procure weapons and dual use technologies (for both Hezbollah and Iran), and conduct operations.

Investigators in several countries have concluded independently that security services should avoid looking for cells that are strictly engaged in fundraising, logistical support, or terrorist operations. Indeed, cells known only to have raised funds have later been found to have played active roles in operations, as was the case, for example, in the 1992 and 1994 suicide bombings in Argentina.

In the words of one U.S. government official, "*Hezbollah cells are always a bit operational.*" Indeed, Hezbollah has conducted a wide variety of operations targeting not only Israeli and Jewish targets, but also the United States. Typically, academics opine that Hezbollah has not targeting the United States since it bombed the U.S. embassy and marine barracks in the 1980's. In fact, there are several more recent instances of Hezbollah activity targeting the U.S., consider the following sampling.

In 1989, Bassam Gharib Makki collected intelligence on Israeli, Jewish and American targets in Germany. In 1989 and 1990, authorities caught a Hezbollah cell operating in Valencia, Spain. The cell was caught smuggling weapons in a ship from Cyprus so they could be pre-positioned and cached in Europe. After tracking that shipment, authorities found additional explosives that had already been stashed in Europe. The cell was determined to have been targeting U.S. and Israeli targets in Europe. In 1997, Hezbollah was found to be collecting intelligence on the U.S. embassy in Nicosia, Cyprus. Throughout the mid- to late-1990s, Hezbollah recruited Palestinian students studying in Russia, and collected intelligence on Israeli, Jewish and American targets there.

Throughout the 1990s, Hezbollah members were active in Singapore, recruiting local Sunnis, collecting intelligence on Israeli and U.S. ships in the Malacca

Straits, and planning attacks. Authorities there uncovered a suicide speed-boat attack very similar to the one that was foiled about a year after September 11 off Gibraltar. Hezbollah is well known for several international attacks, most notably the 1992 and 1994 suicide bombings of the Israeli embassy and Jewish community center (AMIA) respectively in Argentina and the 1995 Khobar Towers attack in Saudi Arabia.

Operations Abroad

Since its founding in 1982, Hezbollah conducts, aside from its activity in Lebanon, a global strategy consisting of setting up operational apparatuses throughout the world and carrying out attacks against Israeli and US targets. Hezbollah has been thus active in a variety of arenas, while focusing on South America, Southeast Asia, Jordan, the Persian Gulf, and the European continent.

During the 1980s, Hezbollah was behind a series of attacks against Western targets, congruent with the policy dictated by Iran. In the 1990s, following a shift in Iranian policy, Hezbollah lowered the profile of its anti-Western pursuits and focused its attention on activity against Israeli and Jewish targets, while availing itself of its worldwide apparatus.

Hezbollah has built up its capacity for carrying out attacks worldwide through its operational wing, which specializes in global terrorist activity. This wing, the so-called "Islamic Jihad", operates branches throughout the world and is headed by Imad Mughniyah, Hassan Nasrallah's military second-in-command.

Hezbollah makes considerable efforts to promote its image, in particular since the September 11 attacks, in order to blur its identity as a terrorist organization. It publicly denies its involvement in terrorism in general, and the existence of a specific apparatus of global terrorism, in particular. At the same time, it continues to build up its strategic operational apparatus abroad.

This apparatus consists of a network of latent operatives, local safe houses, and storage depots of arms and explosives, spread over a large number of countries worldwide. This operational infrastructure is meant to carry out spectacular terrorist attacks against Israeli, Jewish, and US targets worldwide, on short notice upon receiving the order from the organization's leadership or from Iran, and in retaliation for extreme developments in Lebanon or the Palestinian territories.

Hezbollah has a formidable history of activity against Western objectives. During the 1980s, it carried out terrorist attacks against US as well as European targets in Lebanon and abroad. These included a series of bombings in France and a number of kidnappings of US and European civilians and French, British, German, and Russian diplomats. The latter activity was intended to exert pressure for the release of Hezbollah operatives held captive in various countries worldwide. Hezbollah is responsible for most of the kidnappings of foreign nationals carried out in Lebanon during the 1980s and until the beginning of the 1990s. During that period, no less than 18 citizens of Western countries were held hostage under harsh conditions, and three of them were killed.

In the first half of the 1990s, Hezbollah carried out two terrorist attacks in Argentina, evidencing outstanding operational abilities. In May 1999, the Argentinian Supreme Court, upon completion of the official investigation, charged Hezbollah with the bombing of the Israeli Embassy in Buenos Aires on March 17, 1992 and issued a warrant for the arrest of Imad Mughniyah, a terrorist wanted by the United States since the September 11 attacks, for his involvement in terrorist activity during the 1980s.

Argentina

In January 2003, SIDE, the Argentinian intelligence service, issued a 150-page report summarizing its findings on the responsibility of Iran and Hezbollah in the bombing of the Jewish community (AMIA) building in Buenos Aires. The attack was carried out in July 1994 and claimed the lives of 86 people. The SIDE report provides the evidential basis for the report issued by Judge Juan Jose Galiano, who was assigned to the case, and for further investigation of the affair. This report, parts of which were leaked to the press, charges Iran (including its leader, Ayatollah Ali Khamenei, and its former Intelligence Minister, Ali Fallahian) and Hezbollah with direct responsibility for the bombing.

The report refers to Imad Mughniyah (a current member of the Decision-Making Shura Council and head of Hezbollah's military wing) as head of the special operations unit (the so-called "Islamic Jihad") assigned by Iranian intelligence to carry out the bombing as its "sub-contractor". The report includes transcripts of recorded phone calls made by officials of the Iranian embassy in Buenos Aires with Hezbollah operatives and others. It also mentions the contacts established by Iran and Hezbollah with Shiite collaborators in the tri-border area (Brazil, Argentina and Paraguay), who assisted in carrying out the bombing.

The Meeting

Miguel Angel Toma, head of the Argentinian intelligence services (SIDE), visited Israel and met with head of the Mossad Meir Dagan and senior Foreign Ministry officials. The purpose of Toma's four-day visit was to present his Israeli counterparts with a copy of a top-secret report.

The report in question directly implicates Iran, its senior leaders, its intelligence services, and the Hezbollah organization in the July 1994 bombing of the AMIA building, the Center of the Jewish Community in Buenos Aires, in which 85 people were killed and hundreds were wounded. The SIDE report mentions, albeit in passing, that the same pattern of operation and level of command—the Iranian leadership, Iranian intelligence, and Hezbollah—had been behind the bombing of the Israeli embassy in Buenos Aires in March 1992, in which 29 people were killed and dozens injured.

The extensive report, several thousand pages long, includes appendices, transcripts of investigations and phone calls, and border control records. It also mentions names of dozens of Iranian government officials, diplomats, and intelligence officers, as well as Hezbollah operatives and Argentinian and other South American collaborators and auxiliaries involved in initiating, planning, and carrying out the AMIA bombing. The report is based on eight years of intensive investigation conducted with the assistance and participation of the Israeli Mossad, the United States CIA, and other intelligence services.

Dagan and senior Foreign Ministry officials labeled the report "professional, in-depth, and courageous". Toma, a senior member of the Peronist party, though a political appointee and only one year in office, has shown the courage to point the accusing finger at those identified as responsible for the murderous attack.

The list comprises at least twenty-three names, including Ali Khamenei, Iran's leader who, by virtue of his post, has been also in charge of its intelligence services, and numerous Iranian intelligence officers and diplomats, including Iran's then-ambassador to Argentina. It also mentions Imad Mughniyah, the alleged "operations officer" of Hezbollah and head of its special operations unit —the so-called "Islamic Jihad"—who is closely connected to Iranian intelligence.

Mughniyah, who was behind the TWA hijacking in Beirut in 1985 and the kidnappings of Western hostages in Lebanon during the 1980s, features on the US list of most wanted terrorists published by the FBI in the wake of the September 11 attacks.

Although the report in fact reiterates Israeli intelligence allegations that both bombings were the work of Iranian intelligence assisted by Hezbollah, this is the first time that a non-Israeli and non-Jewish authority asserts in such unequivocal terms that Iranian leaders and intelligence officers initiated and perpetrated terrorist attacks.

The report contains records of border control registrations, evidencing that Iranian diplomats and government officials entered and left Argentina under aliases close to the time of the AMIA bombing. It also contains transcripts of recordings of phone calls made by the Iranian embassies in Argentina and neighboring countries to alleged operatives of Hezbollah. In addition, it uncovers links between Iran, Hezbollah, and collaborators residing in the region of Ciudad del Este in the tri-border area of Argentina, Brazil and Paraguay, a region known to house a large concentration of Shiite Muslim immigrants.

The report also refers to the secret testimony given by Abdolghassem Mesbahi, a senior Iranian intelligence officer who defected to Germany in 1996. According to this testimony—a 100-page document, parts of which were published by the New York Times—the decision for both bombings was made by none other than Iranian leader Ali Khamenei and then-President Hashemi Rafsanjani – both of whom also supervised and financed the operation.

Both, defector Mesbahi's testimony and the SIDE report mention that the preparations for the bombings took a long time and necessitated meticulous planning in order to avoid leaving any fingerprints and risk the uncovering of the perpetrators.

After the Iranian leaders endorsed the decision and allocated the required funding, Intelligence Minister Ali Fallahian was appointed to be in charge of the operation. Iranian intelligence approached Hezbollah to act as its sub-contractor in carrying out the bombings. The operational responsibility was assigned to Imad Mughniyah, assisted by intelligence officers who had been posted at the Iranian embassies in the region and the local network of collaborators and supporters.

According to the SIDE report, the bombings were inspired by ideological-religious motives of hostility toward Israel and the Jewish people, and also by political motives.

The essence of the latter was to "punish" the Carlos Menem regime for violating a commitment given by his predecessor President Raul Alfonsín to supply Iran with know-how and equipment needed for setting up the nuclear reactors in Bushehr, including the installing of a heavy water pool. The choice of Argentina as target was facilitated by the presence of a sizeable Jewish community, and the fact that the tri-border area is home to a pro-Iranian and Hezbollah-supporting community, from which collaborators could have easily been recruited.

The proximity of the timings to incidents occurring in the Middle East indicates that both bombings also coincided with vengeful feelings on the part of Hezbollah. The pretext for the bombing of the embassy was the killing of Hezbollah Secretary General Abbas Musawi by Israeli combat helicopters in southern Lebanon. The bombing of the AMIA building occurred shortly after the abduction to Israel of Mustafa Dirani, a senior Shiite officer with close links to Iran and Hezbollah, who captured and detained the Israeli air force navigator Ron Arad.

Based on the SIDE report and an independent inquiry, Argentinian Investigating Judge Juan José Galiano issued international arrest warrants in respect of four Iranian officials: former Intelligence Minister Ali Fallahian, already sought by German authorities in connection with the murder of dissident Iranians; Ali Balesh Abadi, a courier for Iranian intelligence; Mohsen Rabbani, an Iranian intelligence envoy posted under the cover of "cultural attaché" at the Iranian embassy in Buenos Aires, and designated in the report as the "operations officer" of the bombing; and Ali Akbar Parvaresh, former Education Minister and Deputy Speaker of the Iranian Parliament. The latter three visited Argentina a short time before and at the time of the bombing, and left the country immediately afterwards.

Judge Galiano's report quotes the SIDE report in stating that the bombing was carried out by "armed units" of Hezbollah. It does not, however, demand the arrest of any of Hezbollah's operatives. Judge Galiano is also hesitant to directly implicate the Iranian leadership, and chooses to refer, in the explanatory notes accompanying his request to issue arrest warrants, to "radical circles" in Iran.

These formulations exacerbate the suspicion that Judge Galiano arouses among Jews in Argentina. The Jewish community has already accused him and the country's legal system of conducting an indecisive policy of cover-ups and disinformation, following the disappearance of important documents pertaining to the investigation and incidents where vital witnesses failed to appear before the court.

The general mood was also affected by allegations made by the Iranian defector Mesbahi and published by the New York Times. According to these allegations, former President Carlos Menem received $10 million in bribery from a secret bank account in Switzerland controlled by Khamenei and the son of former supreme leader Ayatollah Khomeini, in order to smother the investigation. Menem threatened to file a libel suit against the newspaper.

The relatives of the victims claim that, even though the SIDE report is an important document, it has shifted attention away from the Argentinian scene towards the international arena: it turns the focus away from the collaborators, among whom are police officers who may have known about the impending bombing and did nothing to impede it. During the past few months, a lawsuit is being brought against twenty people suspected of collaboration, mainly in connection with the purchase of the bomb car.

Most of these suspects are criminals and some of them are former police officers. In spite of the above, the Israeli Foreign Ministry already communicated its appreciation to the Argentinian government for its courageous stance. The Iranian government, on its part, denies the allegations against it. It also warned, in a strongly worded conversation with the Argentinian chargé d'affaires at the embassy in Tehran, that pursuing what it defines as a "smear campaign" will lead to the deterioration of relations between the two countries.

Despite Hezbollah's reluctance in recent years to carry out terrorist activity outside Lebanon, it maintains its readiness to carry out such attacks, once a decision is made, and builds up its operational capability to this effect. Hezbollah's operational-terrorist capability constitutes a potential weapon in the hands of the Iranian and Syrian regimes, which they can utilize in the future in line with "strategic considerations.

Israel / Palestine

In recent years, and in particular since the pullout of the Israeli army from Lebanon, Hezbollah has clearly focused its activity on targets in Israel and the Palestinian territories. It has even harnessed its overseas operational apparatus for this purpose, and dispatched operatives via Europe to carry out operational missions on Israeli territory. These missions include gathering operational intelligence, dealing with explosives and arms, and even attempting to carry out attacks.

The following are a few episodes uncovered in Israel, evidencing the way in which Hezbollah exploits the European continent as an operational platform for preparing and launching terrorist attacks on Israeli territory:

- Hussein Mikdad, a Shiite Lebanese citizen and Hezbollah operative, was sent from Lebanon to Israel presumably in order to carry out a "high-quality terrorist attack" on Israeli territory. Mikdad flew from Syria to Austria and traveled by train to Switzerland. He stayed a few days in Hotel Regina in Zurich together with his handler, who prepared him for his entry into Israel. Mikdad entered Israel via Ben-Gurion Airport, using a forged British passport. He spent several days in Tel Aviv and subsequently in Jerusalem, and was seriously injured while assembling an explosive charge in his hotel room at the Lawrence Hotel.

- Stefan Smirak, a young German who converted to Islam in 1994, made up his mind to become a shahid, or martyr, by committing a suicide attack in Israel. To achieve this end, in August 1997 Smirak approached a Hezbollah operative in Germany, who referred him to the Hezbollah headquarters of overseas terrorist activity in Lebanon. In November 1997, Smirak boarded a flight from Amsterdam bound for Tel Aviv. Upon his arrival in Israel, he was supposed to collect an explosive charge in order to carry out a suicide bombing.

Fawzi Ayub is a Lebanese Shiite of Canadian nationality, and an operative of Hezbollah's apparatus of overseas terrorist activity. Ayub left Lebanon for Europe in October 2000, on his Canadian passport. Upon his arrival in Europe, he left his passport behind and purchased new personal belongings to conceal his Lebanese origin. He met with a Hezbollah operative, who supplied him with a forged US passport for his entry into Israel. Ayub stayed in Jerusalem, attempted to approach arms brokers, and was arrested in Hebron by the Palestinian police. In June 2002, following an Israeli military operation in Hebron, Ayub was apprehended by the Israeli security forces. The purpose of his stay in Israel was thus far not uncovered. It is assumed that he intended either to carry out a spectacular bombing, or gather operational intelligence on "high-quality" targets in Israel. Another likely purpose was his infiltration in order to set up an apparatus for future terrorist activity in Israel and the Palestinian territories.

Jihad Shuman, a Lebanese Shiite and Hezbollah operative of British nationality, entered Israel in January 2001. Shuman flew from Lebanon to the United Kingdom on his Lebanese passport, which he was instructed to leave in a hiding place for its collection by another Hezbollah operative. Shuman availed himself of the Hezbollah apparatus in the United Kingdom, and flew to Israel on his authentic British passport. He stayed in Jerusalem, presumably, among other purposes, on a mission of operational intelligence for a terrorist attack in Israel.

Germany

In January 1987, Muhammad Hamade, brother of senior Hezbollah operative Abdel Hadi Hamade, was arrested in Germany while attempting to smuggle containers of liquid explosives camouflaged in three large bottles of arrack. During his interrogation, Hamade revealed the existence of several storage depots of arms near the French-German border. Following his arrest, Hezbollah carried out several terrorist attacks against German targets, including the kidnapping of two German nationals in Lebanon.

Some two years later, in March 1989, the German authorities arrested Bassam Garib Makki, a Hezbollah operative and student in Germany. Makki was found to have in his possession documents containing operational intelligence on Israeli, Jewish, and US targets in Germany that had been targeted for terrorist attacks. He also held operational intelligence on other (British, French, Iraqi, Saudi, and Kuwaiti) objectives, designated as potential targets. The search carried out in his flat in Darmstadt revealed items associated with terrorist activity, such as instructions in Arabic for the preparation and use of explosive charges.

In the bombing of the Mykonos restaurant in Berlin in September 1992, four senior members of the Iranian Kurdish Democratic Party were killed and others were injured. The attack was initiated by the Iranian Intelligence Ministry, one of whose officials presumably recruited two operatives of the Hezbollah cell in Germany with whom he was acquainted, and who assisted in carrying out the bombing.

Spain

In November 1989, a Hezbollah cell, comprised of Hezbollah operatives and local collaborators, was uncovered in the Spanish town of Valencia. The uncovering occurred after a large cache of arms—including explosives and detonators—was found on board a ship that had arrived from Lebanon via Cyprus. The members of the cell were arrested, and additional arms were found in their homes. During their interrogation, they admitted their intention to use these arms in order to carry out terrorist attacks against Israeli and US targets in Europe.

France

In March 1987, French authorities arrested the members of a terrorist network headed by Paris-born Fouad Saleh, who had received military training in Iran in 1981-1982. The arrest led to the uncovering of a widespread operational apparatus that had been responsible for 13 terrorist attacks in France, most of them in the Paris Metro, in all of which Hezbollah operatives were involved. In 1989, Hezbollah devised a scheme of carrying out suicide attacks using small aircraft crashing onto French ships. Iran trained a number of Hezbollah operatives to fly small, single-engine aircraft for this purpose.

United Kingdom

Mustafa Maza, a Hezbollah operative, was killed in August 1989 in a London hotel, when the luggage in his possession exploded.

Cyprus

In 1986, Cypriot security forces arrested two Hezbollah operatives in Larnaca, after they were found in possession of weapons and explosives. In 1997, a Hezbollah unit collected operational intelligence on the US Embassy in Nicosia. Meanwhile, Hezbollah continues to engage in terrorist operations around the globe at a pace not seen since the late 1980s. Hussam Yacoub, a Swedish Hezbollah operative, now in prison, who carried out surveillance of Israeli tourists arriving in Cyprus, calmly explained to Cypriot police that his actions were standard Hezbollah practice, not acts of terrorism. "I don't believe that the missions I executed in Cyprus were connected with the preparation of a terrorist attack in Cyprus. It was just collecting information about the Jews, and this is what my organization is doing everywhere in the world."

Rusia

In September 1985, Hezbollah kidnapped four Soviet diplomats in Lebanon. The kidnappers demanded that the Soviet Union exert pressure on Syria to stop the military activities of pro-Syrian organizations against an Islamic movement in Tripoli. The Soviet diplomats were set free following PLO leader Yasser Arafat's intervention.

Between 1995 and 1999, Hezbollah recruited Palestinian students in Russia for the purpose of setting up an operational apparatus for terrorist activity. The students collected operational intelligence on Israeli and Jewish institutions in Russia, focusing mainly on the Israeli embassy in Moscow. They were also instructed to gather intelligence on US institutions in Moscow.

Italy

In November 1984, a Hezbollah operative was arrested upon his arrival from Lebanon to Switzerland, after he had been found in possession of arms. His arrest led to the uncovering of an operational network comprised of Lebanese students, who had planned an attack against the US embassy in Rome.

Jordan

As part of its endeavors to support Palestinian violent activity, Hezbollah engages in the smuggling of "high-quality" military hardware into the Palestinian territories and Israel via Jordan. At the end of June 2001, Jordanian security forces arrested three members of Hezbollah's operational unit specializing in overseas terrorist activity. The operatives were caught transporting 25 rockets of 107 mm caliber, which had been transferred from Lebanon via Syria to Jordan and were obviously intended to reach the Palestinian territories. The three men were released from Jordanian prison in May 2002 and returned to Lebanon.

Singapore

In 1995, Hezbollah set up a terrorist cell in Singapore with the intention of attacking US and Israeli targets on the island. Hezbollah operatives, who had traveled from Lebanon to Singapore, recruited five Muslims among the local population to operate the cell. The cell's mission was to launch explosive boats against US and Israeli ships passing through or anchoring in the Singapore Straits, based on relevant operational intelligence. The operatives also took pictures of the US and Israeli embassies in Singapore.

Philippines and Malaysia

Pandu Yudhawinata, an Indonesian Hezbollah operative, was arrested in 1999 at the Manila city airport in the Philippines. During his interrogation, he revealed Hezbollah's intentions to recruit Malaysians and Indonesians in order to carry out terrorist attacks in Australia and in Israel.

On the morning of March 11, 1994, a truck coming out of a department store's underground garage hit a motorcycle taxi in the Lumpini neighbourhood of Bangkok. The driver of the motorcycle had just unknowingly foiled a suicide attack on the Israeli embassy a mere 240 metres away. However, it would not be discovered until five years later, after the arrest of Pandu Yudhawinata, a man of Indonesian descent, that this was a Hezbollah attack, almost a year in the making.

Pandu's involvement with Hezbollah can be traced back to as early as 1981, when he was expelled from university for his Islamic activism in Indonesia and fled to Iran. For two years he received military, ideological and language training, before he was sent back to Indonesia to participate in mainstream activism and demonstrations against the Indonesian government. Pandu admitted to Philippine authorities that he was recruited by and worked for Iranian intelligence in Malaysia, before he was recruited to Hezbollah.

It was then he began working for a man with many names, including Abu al-Ful, who Philippine intelligence identified "as the leader of the Islamic Jihad [Organisation], a special attack unit of Hezbollah in south-east Asia." Investigators soon found more skeletons in Pandu's closet, including links to a series of bombing attacks in 1985-87.

Pandu's arrest revealed further Hezbollah plans in south-east Asia. Called the "Five Contingency Plans," they included a maritime bombing plot targeting US Navy and Israeli merchant ships either docking in Singapore or sailing through the Malacca Straits. "The plan," investigators in Singapore determined, "was to use a small boat packed with explosives and ram it into the target vessel."

Hezbollah acquired forged passports in the Philippines for a group of Indonesian recruits it planned to have infiltrate Israel by travelling through Australia, but Pandu's arrest foiled that plot. Another plan included sending operatives to Australia where, it was mistakenly believed, they could acquire legitimate Australian passports in the hopes they would appear less suspicious travelling on documents from a Western country friendly to Israel. It also considered sending three Indonesian members to Australia for a notional attack -- never acted upon -- on American and Jewish targets during the 2000 Olympics.

Tri-lateral cooperation between the United States, Israel, and the Philippines led to the arrest of a senior Hezbollah operative based in Malaysia, who had planned to Southeast Asia.

Hezbollah activity has even reached the United States, the country that defined it as a dangerous terrorist organization, and which suffered hundreds of casualties in its murderous bombings in Lebanon. In July 2000, 23 people suspected of supporting Hezbollah were arrested in North Carolina. They were accused, among other things, of providing assistance to terrorist organizations and of money-laundering activities. Like Hamas and other Middle Eastern terrorist organizations, Hezbollah conducts fundraising activities in the United

States .**Bulgaria**

On July 18, 2012, a bomb exploded in one of the seven buses escorting a group of Israelis just arriving in Burgas, Bulgaria, to enjoy a leisurely vacation. The explosion left the Bulgarian bus driver and five Israelis dead and 30 others wounded. None of the travelers in the large group had noticed when a Caucasian man in Bermuda shorts and a T-shirt, wearing a baseball cap and glasses, and carrying a backpack, joined the crowd in the airport terminal and walked with them to the buses.

At the time, he wore a long, blond wig, but a rental clerk would recognize him from a surveillance video, recalling that he spoke English with an Arabic accent, had short hair, carried a wad of 500-euro notes, and seemed upset when he had rented a car.

After six months of investigation, Bulgarian authorities discovered the Canadian bomber's handlers were 25-year-old Canadian citizen Hassan al-Hajj Hassan and 32-year-old Meliad Farah, also known as Hussein Hussein, an Australian citizen. Both reportedly escaped back to Lebanon after the bombing in Bulgaria and are allegedly hiding in southern Lebanon. They are now on trial (in absentia) in Bulgaria for their suspected involvement in the bombing; both are of Lebanese origin and are members of Hezbollah. According to Israeli officials, the Burgas bomber, whose full identity is unknown but was related to the Canadian co-conspirator, according to DNA tests, was selected in part because he was not Lebanese "in order to avoid any suspicions."

This case of Hezbollah recruiting and using operatives of dual citizenship to carry out attacks is not unique to the men involved in the Burgas bombing. In fact, this fits a pattern Hezbollah has long employed, of recruiting operatives with Western complexions, nationalities and passports, and then using these recruits to carry out operations abroad.

Thailand

In January 2012, Thai police arrested such an agent, Hussein Atris, a dual Swedish-Lebanese citizen with a Swedish passport, trying to flee the country. Intelligence officials surmised Hezbollah had been using Thailand as an explosives hub -- Atris rented the space a year earlier -- and decided to use its on-hand operatives and material to target Israeli tourists. He has since been sentenced by Thai authorities for possession of explosive materials. But Atris is only a recent example of a Hezbollah operative working -- and getting caught -- in south-east Asia, a region they have been active in for the past few decades.

Equipment

Hezbollah has long maintained a particularly active weapons-procurement effort in Canada. Not only does the group have a significant pool of members, supporters and sympathizers in Canada, but the country's strong position in industry, trade, and finance make it an attractive place to procure dual-use items.

The immigration case of Mohammad Hussein al Hussein, who was ultimately ordered deported from Canada in 1994, sheds significant light on Hezbollah's presence in the country. Interviewed by Canadian security officials, al Husseini provided information both on Hezbollah attacks abroad and on the group's presence and activities in Canada. He specified that "Hezbollah has members in Montreal, Ottawa, Toronto -- in all of Canada." Referring to the situation in Montreal, al Husseini implied that he could provide Canadian authorities information about cigarette and weapons smuggling if the Canadian government would cut a deal with him.

Mohammad Hassan Dbouk and his brother-in-law, Ali Adham Amhaz, ran the Canadian portion of Hezbollah's funding and procurement network under the command of Haj Hassan Hilu Laqis (then Hezbollah's chief military procurement officer). Their activities were funded in part with money that Laqis sent from Lebanon, in addition to their own criminal activities in Canada.

Under the win-win scam, they procured materials for Hezbollah and still made a profit: While their credit card and bank frauds covered the cost of the items they bought for Hezbollah, they still received 50 cents on the dollar from Laqis for the materials they procured.

The items that the Hezbollah procurement network purchased or discussed purchasing in North America for smuggling into Lebanon were used, according to a defense specialist who served as an expert witness, to increase Hezbollah's tactical capabilities on the battlefield. Commander James Campbell, a former U.S. Defense Intelligence Agency counterterrorism intelligence officer, said the list was ambitious and indicative of Hezbollah's increasing military sophistication: night-vision devices (goggles, cameras, and scopes), surveying equipment, global positioning systems (watches and aviation antennas), mine and metal detection equipment, camera and video equipment, advanced aircraft analysis and design software, and a variety of computer equipment including laptops, high-speed modems, processors, joysticks, plotters, scanners, and printers.

North Carolina

Commander Campbell pointed out to a jury several video clips -- from videos seized at the home of Mohammad Hammoud, a convicted Hezbollah member who is now serving time in a North Carolina prison -- of Hezbollah militants using the kind of equipment Dbouk's network procured for Hezbollah in Canada. Such examples were not coincidental, given that Hezbollah sought specific items its fighters needed in the field. For example, the procurement network was asked to send specific compasses because "the guys were getting lost, you know, in the woods, or whatever, and they need compasses."

In one instance, Said Harb, another convicted member of the North Carolina Hezbollah-support cell, provided Dbouk with $4,000 toward the purchase of such items. As Harb later recalled in testimony, Dbouk once asked him, when the two met in Canada: "Would you like to get anything, you know, for the guys?" Instructed to explain this more clearly, Harb elaborated: "*We were talking about Hezbollah. Hezbollah has social, military, political, different branches within Hezbollah. We were talking about the military branch. You know, The Resistance.*"

In support of its procurement efforts for "the Resistance," the Canadian Hezbollah network considered supplementing its income through other schemes, including importing counterfeit $100 bills from Lebanon. But the network already had more money than it needed through basic credit card bust-out schemes.

The Hezbollah network also considered trying to take out a life insurance policy in Canada for a prospective Hezbollah fighter in Lebanon who might be killed carrying out a suicide attack, or otherwise engaging in combat from which he would not return. Concerned a Canadian insurance company would not honor the policy of a suicide bomber, Dbouk suggests a death certificate could be produced falsely claiming the person was a civilian killed while "sitting in his village."

In the years since Hezbollah's 2006 war with Israel, Hezbollah's procurement program has taken on renewed importance as the group has spent much of its time replenishing its weapons stocks. Big-ticket items, like missiles, have been provided by Iran and sometimes Syria. But other items, from small arms and ammunition to shoulder-fired rockets and dual use items, are also procured globally through Hezbollah networks. According to Sheikh Nabil Qaouq, a Hezbollah commander in southern Lebanon, "*the resistance is using this period to prepare, to train, to strengthen capabilities, and the enemy itself can attest to this.*"

Speaking in December 2011, Hezbollah leader Hassan Nasrallah himself underscored the group's procurement efforts. "*We will never let go of our arms*," he said. "*Our numbers are increasing day after day, and we are getting better and our training is becoming better and we are becoming more confident in our future and more armed. And if someone is betting that our weapons are rusting, we tell them that every weapon that rusts is replaced.*"

In 2001, Mohammad Dbouk was indicted in U.S. federal court under Operation Smokescreen. According to U.S. investigators, Dbouk is an Iranian-trained Hezbollah operative and "*an intelligence specialist and propagandist [who] was dispatched to Canada by Hezbollah for the express purpose of obtaining surveillance equipment.*" According to information collected by the Canadian Security Intelligence Service (CSIS) during its investigation into Mohammad Dbouk's activities in Canada, first in Montreal and then in Vancouver, Dbouk was acting under the direction of Hezbollah's then chief of procurement, the aforementioned Haj Hassan Hilu Laqis, who was based in Lebanon. Mohammad Dbouk reportedly lived in the Detroit area for about six months, taking his activities to the U.S. side of the Ambassador Bridge linking Michigan and Ontario.

Dbouk solicited the assistance of his friend Said Harb to help facilitate the purchase of dual-use equipment and to test a scheme to use counterfeit credit cards to purchase these materials. According to CSIS intercepts, in 1999 Dbouk informed an unidentified male that he had known Harb for more than 15 years and that the two had been jailed and beaten together (presumably during the Lebanese civil war). Harb was already at the center of a laundry list of criminal enterprises and frauds, but it was his relationship with Dbouk that brought him to the attention of CSIS agents who were already monitoring Dbouk's activities.

U.S. Attorney Robert Conrad, whose office successfully prosecuted the Hezbollah case in Charlotte, testified before the U.S. Congress that according to intelligence he'd examined, "*Dbouk is such a major player in the Hezbollah organization that on five separate occasions his application to be a martyr was rejected.*" Given his overall intelligence, his military training, and his expertise in information operations, Dbouk was too valuable a commodity to expend on a martyrdom mission.

Dbouk appears to have accepted Hezbollah's refusal to send him on a martyrdom mission, and dove into his procurement responsibilities in an attempt to secure a place in heaven through devotion to his assigned task.

According to the CSIS intercepts, in a conversation with someone named Said (last name unknown), Dbouk tried to discuss politics; but Said said he wanted to be careful about what they discussed on the telephone. Ignoring the kind of operational security protocol for which Hezbollah is well known, Dbouk responded that "*he did not care about anything and was committed to securing all the items for the brothers at any cost; he was attempting to avoid going to hell and secure a place in heaven by so doing.*"

Hezbollah in Syria

As the war in Syria rages, the conflict has presented a major challenge to Lebanese Hizballah's military organization, command, and combat forces. Hizballah has embarked on sustained expeditionary warfare for the first time in its history and finds itself pitted against enemies it had neither sought nor prepared to fight, on unfamiliar territory, and in a cause different from its "resistance" raison d'etre.

The war in Syria has not been easy for the group, and the conflict shines a light on Hizballah's combat performance and capabilities. Hizballah is gaining valuable knowledge of irregular warfare and actual combat experience, but this may have only limited relevance in a future conflict with Israel.

The high reported number of Hizballah forces estimated to have been committed to Syria is about 10,000, but this likely reflects the total rotated through Syria, not the number present at any one time.

The French foreign minister provided a more reasonable estimate of 3,000-4,000 in May 2013 during the height of the battle in Qusayr. In September 2013, Reuters cited "regional security officials" as providing an estimate of 2,000-4,000. Types of units and troops sent to Syria include "elite and special forces," and "reservists."

Based on videos of purported Hizballah combatants in Syria, they resemble regular soldiers. They are uniformed, have load bearing equipment, and in some cases wear protective vests. Weapons and equipment also seen with purported Hizballah forces in Syria include standard light infantry weapons (assault rifles, general purpose machine-guns), anti-tank guided missiles (ATGM) and rocket-propelled grenades (RPG), truck-mounted heavy machine guns ("Dushkas"), light mortars, and recoilless rifles.

Hizballah reportedly operated regime armored vehicles in the fighting in Qusayr, but this was likely a situation in which Hizballah forces were operating with regime regular armored units.

The organization of Hizballah forces in Syria is unclear. One report, citing a "regional security source," indicated that Hizballah functions with a command structure including Islamic Revolutionary Guard Corps (IRGC) and Syrian Army personnel and has been given specific geographic areas of responsibility. Based on the different geographic fronts where they are fighting, Hizballah forces are probably organized on a territorial basis with separate commands for forces in Damascus and its suburbs, Aleppo city and Aleppo Province, and Homs Province.

Hizb allah is one component of the diverse forces mobilized by the regime. These forces include: regime regulars from the army, air force, air defense force, and navy; irregular forces of the National Defense Force (NDF) allied forces from Iraq; and possibly some Iranian combat forces in small numbers.

Hizballah has brought important capabilities to the war on the regime's side. Its forces in Syria are essentially light infantry that can be depended on to execute both offensive and defensive missions in areas important to the regime. They have learned to cooperate with regime heavy forces including armor, artillery, and air units, and to work effectively with regime irregulars and allies.

Based largely on opposition reporting, Hizballah has been involved in direct combat and corseting operations in eight areas within Syria, and in corseting and advisory operations in three more. Reports posted by Syrian opposition elements reveal more than 80 specific locations where Hizballah is said to have been involved in military actions.

Kill Mughniyeh

Imad Mughniyeh was born in 1962 in the Lebanese Shi'ite village of Tayr Dibba to a poor family of olive and lemon harvesters. He moved to Beirut as a child and despite his religious affiliation, he became active in the predominantly Sunni Palestinian al-Fatah movement.

In Lebanese Palestinian reports, Mughniyeh was even described as participating in the unit of bodyguards protecting then-PLO chief Yasser Arafat. But after the PLO chairman and his fighters were forced to leave Lebanon following the Israeli invasion in 1982 – just three years after the Islamic Revolution in Iran – Mughniyeh returned to his own religious cohort and joined Hezbollah, "The Party of God," a heavily armed Lebanese faction established and nurtured by Iran.

He quickly involved himself in some of the most outrageous Hezbollah attacks, proving his loyalty and his skills. He was trained by the chillingly skilled Iranian Revolutionary Guard Corps.

In a bloody two-year period – between November 1982 and September 1984 – he was a key player in several car bombing attacks against Israeli, American, and French targets in Lebanon. Among his trademarks: videotapes made by the suicide bombers and their accomplices nearby. The terrifying impact was thus magnified.

The attacks of those years included two assaults on Israeli military headquarters in the southern city of Tyre, which killed 150 Israelis and Lebanese. He orchestrated the suicide bombings of the U.S. Marines barracks and a French military building in Beirut, killing 241 American servicemen, 58 French paratroopers, and six Lebanese civilians.

He was also a major actor in the bombing of the 1984 U.S. Embassy in Beirut, which killed 63 people. And this was just the beginning. His career would mushroom over the next two and a half decades.

In 1985, Mughniyeh personally participated in the hijacking of a TWA airliner. After it was forced to land in Beirut, a U.S. Navy diver among the passengers – Robert Stethem – was tortured and killed.

The first image of Mughniyeh, then just 22 years old, was first seen in the pages of the Western press when photographed waving his pistol near the TWA pilot's head in the cockpit. That photo was the key evidence used by U.S. law enforcement officials to indict Mughniyeh for murder in that incident. But for Israel, it would take another seven years to realize his significance.

The Hezbollah man was the architect of the 1992 bombing of the Israeli Embassy in Buenos Aires, Argentina, which killed 29 people – including seven Israelis, among them one Mossad agent. This was Mughniyeh's revenge for the Israeli helicopter attack that had killed Hezbollah's top leader, Abbas Moussawi.

The Buenos Aires attack led Israel to acknowledge two important facts: One, that Mughniyeh would avenge every Israeli attack on his organization; and two, that Mughniyeh had to be wiped out.

These realizations were further strengthened by an attack two years later, when along with his Iranian patrons, Mughniyeh masterminded the bombing of the Jewish community center in the Argentinian capital, which devastated the building and left 85 people dead.

From that point on, Israel used every opportunity it could to try to get rid of Mughniyeh. Numerous tentative plans were drawn up, but only three came into fruition.

In 1994, the Mossad conspired a devious plan to obliterate Mughniyeh: Lebanese agents working for the Mossad planted a car bomb aimed at Mughniyeh's brother Fuad. Anticipating that Mughniyeh would attend his brother's funeral, Israel planned to carry out their assassination of the Hezbollah military chief then: But Imad Mughniyeh, probably paranoid about possible attempts on his life, did not show up at the funeral.

A few months after Fuad's death, Israeli intelligence managed to obtain precise information that Imad Mughniyeh was scheduled to board a flight from Damascus to Tehran using a false name.

The Mossad informed the CIA of Mughniyeh's whereabouts, and the Americans orchestrated a redirection of the flight to Kuwait and dispatched a military plane from Saudi Arabia to bring Mughniyeh to justice in the U.S. courts.

But the CIA made a cardinal error: It disclosed to the Kuwaitis the identity of the wanted terrorist. Fearing retribution from Hezbollah should they accede to the U.S. demand, the Kuwaitis declined to order the passengers of the plane to disembark. Kuwait permitted the flight to take off to Tehran.

The next missed opportunity was completely the Israelis' fault. After the Israeli withdrawal from Lebanon in 2000, the senior echelon of Hezbollah – known as the top five – paraded along the Israeli border on a victorious patrol tour. Mughniyeh was among them.

Israeli reconnaissance photographed the five and transmitted the images to Aman (military intelligence) headquarters in Tel Aviv. They were identified; and an attack plan was put into motion. Drone aircraft that could fire missiles were launched.

Western intelligence sources say they were told by Israelis later that this was a "rare opportunity to disrupt Hezbollah's leadership." But the order to kill never came. Prime Minister Ehud Barak, who was proud of ordering the Israeli withdrawal from south Lebanon after 18 years of occupation, feared that the relative calm would be disrupted if he had Hebzollah's top leaders eliminated.

Senior officers in the Mossad were furious. Years of painstaking information-gathering efforts were wasted. But they had no choice but to accept their political leader's decision and to wait for the next opportunity.

Mughniyeh, as the years went by, became more cautious. Israeli intelligence learned that he went to a plastic surgeon in Beirut to alter his appearance.

He also moved to the safe haven of Tehran, where he enhanced his professional and personal ties with the Revolutionary Guards commanders – particularly with the charismatic General Qassem Soleimani, who was head of the elite Al-Quds force.

After returning to his Beirut headquarters, Mughniyeh continued to travel frequently among the triangle of the capitals of Lebanon, Syria and Iran.

The Mossad hunters, experts in human weaknesses and knowing that nobody is immune to error, waited patiently – but desperately.

Mughniyeh did indeed make mistakes, basically feeling too safe in the Syrian capital. He went to Damascus for both business and pleasure.

For his bloody business, he would meet with his master and friend, Iranian General Soleimani, to coordinate and plot strategy. Often joining them was General Muhammad Suleiman, top security adviser to Syrian President Bashar Assad and the man in charge of the regime's nuclear reactor and its special military ties with Iran and Hezbollah.

After working hours, Mughniyeh would enjoy the pleasures that Damascus had to offer: good food, alcohol and women – most of which he would not risk indulging in back home in the religious Shi'ite neighborhoods of Beirut.

Details of the "operation"

Piecing together human intelligence and telephone intercepts, Israeli intelligence managed to learn a great deal about Mughniyeh's private life and tracked his movements, finally aware of his post-plastic surgery appearance. They took advantage of two human weaknesses, quite uncharacteristic for a master terrorist on the run.

First, hosted by Syrian intelligence in one of its guest apartments, and in constant contact with Iranian "diplomats," Mughniyeh felt totally comfortable in Damascus. Living for decades with the assumption that he was an assassination target, he must have craved a place to feel safe. He let down his guard when in Syria, moving around with full self-confidence and no fear.

He also permitted himself to do, in Damascus, what he did not do at home in Lebanon: fool around with women. That, too, meant that he was literally a man about town, in moving cars more than a cautious man would be. Spies for the Mossad took note of routes that he repeatedly took.

Mughniyeh had an apartment in the posh neighborhood of Kafr Sousa, home to Syria's most wealthy businessmen and the military and intelligence cronies of the Assad regime. Feeling safe and secure due to his altered appearance and years of evading assassination attempts, Mughniyeh would travel in his SUV from Beirut to Damascus without bodyguards, often with his personal driver but sometimes alone.
Mughniyeh and other Hizbullah men lowered their guard and were relaxed while in Damascus, believing that they were beyond Israel's reach. Mughniyeh was walking alone, when a car bomb exploded.

The Mossad recruited a Syrian expat who visited his country often, and asked him to move to Damascus to provide logistics for the operation. The agent provided a villa to hide the vehicle and affix it with explosives, in addition to accommodations for the group that carried out the operation.

He rented the villa in an upscale suburb of Damascus ("Assad Villages"), located to the northwest of Kfar Sousa, and asked an ironsmith to separate the car entrance from the pedestrian entrance with an iron net on three sides, making it look like a cage and blocking the entry to the villa from that location.

A while later, the agent went back to Syria and bought a Mitsubishi Pajero 4×4, after knowing that several similar makes visited the targeted location often. In addition, Mughniyeh sometimes drove the same make. The execution team used a different model, Mitsubishi Lancer, due to its popularity in Syria in general.

The Pajero, now parked in the villa, was equipped with explosives in its trunk door. It was later discovered that, in addition to the explosives, the bomb contained metal pellets that can cause extensive damage to the target instantaneously. The device was similar to several bombs used by Israel to assassinate leaders in Lebanon and abroad.

The investigators and people close to the file are very secretive about the implementation team. But there are indicators that show that they were not Syrian citizens and that they had travelled in and out of the country to implement the operation.

In the early afternoon of 12 February 2008, one of the implementers drove the Pajero, equipped with explosives in its trunk door, and parked it outside the building frequented by Mughniyeh.

At dusk, the team of four individuals took the getaway Lancer and, after making sure that the construction workers had left the building under construction next to Mughniyeh's building, three of them went upstairs to observe the parking lot, the target, and the vehicle with the explosives.

They chose an apartment on the sixth floor. One of them surveyed the area with binoculars, another was charged with detonating the explosives, and the third was for protection. The fourth waited in the getaway car parked at the back of the building close to the fence.

Right before 10:20 pm, Mughniyeh exited the building and, as soon as he reached the well-lit lot nine meters away from the Pajero, the bomb was detonated and he was killed instantly.

Pe'al!" ordered the senior Mossad commander in charge of this extraordinary mission. Translated from Hebrew, this meant Go. Act. Push the button. The expert sitting beside the commander obeyed the order. He pushed the button. One hundred and thirty-five miles (215 km.) away in Syria's capital, Damascus, an explosion tore a notorious terrorist to bits.

The explosion was heard around 10:20 pm. Some people rushed to the location, including those Mughniyeh was seeing in the apartment. It turned out that when Mughniyeh had stepped out of the building's main gate, a 2006 silver Mitsubishi Pajero 4×4 parked nine meters away exploded, killing him alone, on the spot.

The implementing team left the building and headed toward their getaway car. They immediately drove toward the Mazzeh highway where they parked the car on the side of the road and left behind some items for distraction. The investigations showed that the implementing team faced a problem while escaping, which led them to leave the car and use another to escape to an unknown location.

This was a triumph for the men and women of Israeli intelligence. They had accomplished the nearly impossible. Their feeling was similar to the satisfaction Americans would enjoy, three years later, when Navy Seals found and killed Osama bin Laden.

A manhunt lasting a quarter of a century had come to an end. At Mossad headquarters at the Glilot Junction north of Tel Aviv there was great relief and even celebration.

In a most unusual example of operational cooperation, a CIA liaison officer was also in the Mossad HQ – part of the logistics and decision-making process for the assassination. The Israelis understood that officials at CIA headquarters in Langley, Virginia, were also very pleased.

Yet Israelis close to their country's intelligence agencies are telling Western officials something different: that the operation was almost entirely "blue and white" – referring to the colors of Israel's flag – with hardly any "red, white, and blue."

The Israelis were surprised to learn, during strategic talks with their counterparts in Washington, that the Americans were just as eager to get rid of him. Since 1975, the CIA had been forbidden by Congress to carry out assassinations – even of America's worst enemies. But that policy changed after 9/11, when President George W. Bush ordered targeted killings using drone aircraft.

Nevertheless, in the eyes of the Bush administration – though not always understood by the Israelis – there was a huge difference between sending assassins and killing targets from the sky.

At a certain point during consultations with the Americans, then-Mossad director Meir Dagan proposed to his CIA counterpart, Gen. Michael Hayden, a joint operation to eliminate Mughniyeh.

Gen. Michael Hayden (as CIA director under President George W. Bush) agreed, but he set two conditions: First, that no innocent people would be hurt: The Americans were very concerned by the proximity of Mughniyeh's apartment to a girls' school; second, that only Mughniyeh would be targeted – and that none of his Syrian or Iranian acquaintances could be touched. The United States was reluctant to stir up violent conflicts with sovereign states.

At least according to what Israelis have been telling Western officials, the Mossad did not need the CIA for active management of the operation. They had already gleaned all the details necessary about Mughniyeh's daily routine and his hideout in Damascus.

The CIA was there, as they put it, to fill in any missing intelligence information and provide extra eyes in Damascus. The Mossad certainly had its own excellent expertise, in its Kidon (Bayonet) special operations unit, when it came to killing terrorists. Still, the Israelis felt more comfortable having the CIA take part – even if the American role was seen as minor.

As agreed by Dagan and Hayden, a senior CIA official from its operations directorate was assigned to the Mossad team working on the project. The command center was in Tel Aviv.

Kidon operatives, along with Aman signals intelligence Unit 8200, monitored Mughniyeh almost around the clock, zooming in on his safe-house and the parking lot nearby. Based on previous operations, it can be assumed that the team had some physical presence in the area. It was decided that the weapon of choice would be a bomb planted in or on a car parked near Mughniyeh's apartment.

The CIA-Mossad relations hit a bump, for a while, when the Americans got cold feet and pulled out of the operation. The CIA began to reiterate its fears of the collateral damage that such an assassination would cause – concerned, despite Israel's assurances, about the girls' school nearby.

The Mossad was sorry to see the CIA pull out, but the preparations continued. Nevertheless, then-Prime Minister Ehud Olmert ordered the Mossad to make sure that the "killing zone" of the bomb be very narrow, so that only Mughniyeh would be touched.

The "toy factory" of the Mossad and the Aman agency – their technological units – began designing, assembling and testing the bomb. It was a laborious procedure, requiring dozens of tests, until the results were satisfactory and matched the guidelines stipulated by Olmert. The process was filmed, time and again, for analysis and dissection.

Contrary to the recent reports in the American media, the process of developing the bomb was carried out in Israel. Not in the U.S. Once Olmert was confident that the bomb would be highly accurate, officials say they have learned from Israel that Olmert brought the video clips to Washington. He showed them to President Bush and asked him to bring the CIA back into the operation. The video clearly showed that the diameter of the "killing zone" was no more than 10 meters. Bush was impressed. The next day, while he was still in the U.S., Olmert received a call from Dagan informing him that the CIA was back in.

The bomb was smuggled to Syria via Jordan, whose intelligence ties with the CIA and the Mossad had been tight and intimate for decades. The involvement of the CIA gave the Jordanians a sense of security in cooperating, in case of Hezbollah retribution.

There were two main obstacles to executing the operation. Mughniyeh's visits to his Damascus apartment were random and could not be predetermined by the surveillance teams. Secondly, it was difficult for the teams to ensure that they would be able to secure a spot for their rigged car to be parked near Mughniyeh or his vehicle.

Eventually, the conspirators found an undisclosed operational solution which would give them enough warning time ahead of Mughniyeh's arrival to prepare the trap.

The day of the assassination arrived: On the evening of February 12, Mughniyeh's car was spotted pulling into the parking lot. The Mossad planners breathed a sigh of relief. The school nearby was closed for the night. Even if the bomb was unexpectedly flawed, the innocent school girls were not at risk.

But to the agony of the project managers, when the car doors opened, Mughniyeh was not alone: Iranian commander Soleimani and the Syrian nuclear coordinator Suleiman exited the vehicle with him. At the command center in Tel Aviv, the order was given: Hold.

The three buddies went up to the apartment. In Tel Aviv, the Mossad project managers and their CIA liaison waited, nervously biting their nails, on the verge of losing hope. A few hours later, the information arrived that Soleimani and Suleiman had left the apartment and been picked up by a car. The planners could now only pray that Mughniyeh would not remain in the apartment overnight.

About half an hour later, the surveillance team reported that Mughniyeh had entered the parking lot and approached his car.
In Tel Aviv, the order rang out: "Pe'al!The master terrorist, the Hezbollah commander whose trademark was car bombing, fell victim to his own craft in a blast of poetic justice.

Kill Olmert

Mughniyeh's successor, Mustafa Badr Adin, ordered attacks on Israeli embassies and tried to assassinate Olmert and senior Israeli military officers and officials.

But Badr Adin repeatedly failed. His only success was in 2012 at Burgas airport in Bulgaria, when a Hezbollah suicide bomber killed five Israeli tourists and their Bulgarian driver.

Security precautions around Olmert were stepped up last year out of concern that Hezbollah would attempt to get at him. Olmert was in office not only at the time of the Mughniyeh killing but during the month-long war between Israel and Hezbollah in 2006.

Olmert, who is now facing additional corruption charges after being indicted in an Israeli court, is loathed by the majority of Israelis. But analysts who watch the country's security and defense policies believe that in those areas he was far-sighted, showed determination, and was willing to take risks.

In September 2007, just five months before ordering the assassination of Mughniyeh, Olmert unleashed Israel's covert operatives and then the air force to destroy the Syrian nuclear reactor that North Korea had helped build in a remote area.

One can only imagine what the world would look like had the reactor been built and operated in an area now controlled by the brutal Islamic State. Six months after Mughniyeh's assassination, Olmert approved a covert operation in which Israeli long-range snipers – apparently firing from a ship – assassinated Syria's nuclear coordinator, Gen. Suleiman, while he dined with guests on the balcony of his villa overlooking the Mediterranean.

Days after Mughniyeh was killed, then Vice President Dick Cheney called Olmert and they exchanged congratulations for the successful operation. President Bush, too, held Olmert in high respect – reportedly telling someone he liked the Israeli leaders because "he has balls."

The man of Mossad

The alleged Israeli spy who reportedly infiltrated Hezbollah and frustrated attacks against Israel held a number of important positions, including supervising the personal security of the organization's leader, Hassan Nasrallah. The alleged Mossad member was reportedly arrested weeks ago and held the position of deputy chief of Unit 910, which carries out operations against specific Israeli targets.

Mohammed Shawraba was a resident of a village in south Lebanon and comes from a family that includes religious figures known for their loyalty to Hezbollah. But sources added that Mohammed Shawraba arrest would not hurt his family, which "cannot be blamed for his deeds." He reportedly advanced in Hezbollah until he became responsible for Nasrallah's personal security with an emphasis on surveillance.

After the spy was discovered, Hezbollah was quick to discharge the unit's fighters and spread them around to other units. The commander was similarly discharged after the spy reported his activities to US and Israeli intelligence. The espionage involved more than one person – a cell – that was "the most serious [intelligence] breach in Hezbollah's history." Under questioning, it was revealed that Mossad made periodic payments totaling $1 million. Mossad spy worked undercover as a businessman and traveled a great deal.

Mossad allegedly recruited Mohammed Shawraba in a western Asian country. He worked with Mossad for a number of years and foiled many Hezbollah operations that were meant to avenge the assassination of commander Imad Mughniyeh in Damascus in 2008. The double agent also supposedly exposed information about operatives operating abroad, leading to the arrest of Hezbollah agent Muhammad Amadar in Lima, Peru.

The recurring failures of Unit 910 "caused a state of frustration in the party's ranks," and led to the creation of a separate secret unit run by Iran's Revolutionary Guards. After close monitoring of the most important security officials, the unit arrested five Hezbollah members including the [Unit 910 deputy chief]. Hezbollah refuses to deny or confirm reports that Shawraba fed the Mossad intelligence on the Lebanese group's foreign-operations unit, which he had headed since 2008.

He was arrested with four people who worked for him in the group's foreign-operations unit, which works against Israeli interests in foreign countries, the newspaper reported. It said Hezbollah had become suspicious of Shawraba after five attempted retaliations against Israel over the Mughniyeh killing had failed.

The agent, who was arrested earlier this year by Hezbollah's counter-intelligence force, and is now undergoing trial, was able to penetrate the highest levels of the Shiite militant group, and leaked sensitive information to Israel for several years prior to his capture. American newspaper The

Washington Post and Lebanese newspaper The Daily Star cite "security officials and people in Lebanon" who say they are familiar with the incident. They say the agent's activities constitute "one of the most significant security breaches" in the history of Hezbollah, the Shiite militant group that controls large swathes of Lebanese territory.

According to reports from Lebanon, several years ago Shawraba used to direct the personal security detail of Hassan Nasrallah, Hezbollah's secretary-general. Nasrallah has led the militant group since 1992, when his predecessor, Abbas al-Musawi, was assassinated by Israel. In 2008, after a number of years in the service of Nasrallah's personal security detail, Shawraba was promoted to director of the group's Unit for Foreign Operations, also known as Unit 910, which collects information on Israeli activities abroad. However, unbeknownst to Hezbollah officials, Shawraba had been recruited by the Israeli spy agency Mossad even before he joined Nasrallah's personal security team.

According to The Post, the information he shared with the Mossad on a regular basis helped Israel thwart a number of high-profile Hezbollah operations in Lebanon and Israel, especially in 2006. Eventually, however, Hezbollah's military commanders became increasingly suspicious of the high rate of failed operations, and began to suspect that a mole inside the group's senior command structure was feeding sensitive operational information to the Israelis. Eventually, Shawraba was arrested after Hezbollah's leadership was given crucial information from Iranian intelligence sources.

The mole – who the news site said was recruited by Mossad in an Asian country eight years ago – allegedly passed information to Israeli secret services that led to the 2009 assassination of high-ranking Hezbollah official Imad Mughniyah and the 2013 killing of Hassan al-Laqqi. He is also said to have revealed Hezbollah members to the Israelis that led to the arrest of Mohammed Amadar in Peru this year and Hossam Yaacoub in Cyprus last year, as well as Daoud Farhat and Youssef Ayad – detained in April 2014 in Bangkok for allegedly planning attacks against tourists in Thailand.

Hezbollah became suspicious when the Bulgarian Interior Ministry accused it of being behind the 2012 bus bombing in Burgas that killed five Israeli tourists and the bus driver, said the source, who added that Shawraba leaked information to Israel, which then forwarded it to Bulgarian authorities, who had released pictures of the two Hezbollah members suspected of the bombing.

www.ingramcontent.com/pod-product-compliance
Lightning Source LLC
Chambersburg PA
CBHW081605280526
45788CB00011B/3570